INDOOR GARDENING FOR
BROWN THUMBS

# FLOWERING HOUSEPLANTS

by Gary M. Spahl

Illustrated by
Kathleen Estes

BRISTOL PUBLISHING ENTERPRISES
San Leandro, California

Printed in Singapore.

ISBN 1-55867-184-6

# CONTENTS

Look for other books
in this series.

Indoor Gardening For Brown Thumbs

HANGING PLANTS
TOUGHEST HOUSEPLANTS
FLOWERING HOUSEPLANTS
HERBS
LARGE FLOOR PLANTS
PLANTS FOR DARK CORNERS

for a free catalog, call or write

Bristol Publishing Enterprises
800 346-4889
in California
510 895-4461
P.O. Box 1737
San Leandro, CA 94577

## YOU <u>CAN</u> GROW FLOWERING HOUSEPLANTS!

Are you florally challenged? Does your Mother's Day Azalea lose its flowers before Memorial Day? Does your neighbor ask you to stroll through his yard so the dandelions will die? It's okay — let it out. You're not alone. I also was once like you.

We've all purchased or received beautiful flowering plants and then watched the blooms drop off like paratroopers in a matter of days. Well, there are some tricks to caring for flowering houseplants. This book features eight plants I call the Bloomin' Bunch — and it shows you how to keep them bloomin' as long as possible. Just follow the simple instructions on light requirements, watering and fertilizer and you'll be delighted to learn that an Azalea can actually keep its blossoms until Father's Day.

Flowering plants are different than foliage houseplants, and they have different needs. This doesn't mean they're needy. It should only take a few minutes a week to care for them. The secret is caring for them correctly. For example, while most foliage plants like warmer temperatures, many of the Bloomin' Bunch are pretty cool cats. You can give 'em the right amount of water and light, but put them in a warm room, and they're goners.

Flowers make us happy. You've probably heard the advice to buy yourself some flowers if you're feeling low. It works! The bright, natural colors perk up our spirits and lighten our moods. Taking care of flowering plants makes us even happier, because caring for a living thing enriches our own lives. So having flowering plants is like getting a double shot of happiness!

Treat yourself to a couple of the Bloomin' Bunch. And while you're at it, tell your neighbor to invest in some weed killer, because you're going to be florally challenged no more.

# FLOWERING HOUSEPLANTS: THE BLOOMIN' BUNCH

Add cheer to a holiday, brighten a rainy or wintery season, perk up your spirits and add beauty to your room. This group of houseplants is easy to grow; all you need is a little know-how.

Here they are: eight flowering plants with the color and pizzazz of the Ziegfield Follies. Like most flowering plants, the Bloomin' Bunch likes fairly bright light and consistent moisture. Beyond that, these stars are individuals, each with its own personality and blooming seasons. There are delicate plants with soft, fuzzy leaves and dainty flowers, and dramatic plants with striking leaves and flowers that belong in a contemporary art gallery. There are blue flowers and red flowers. Yellow and pink and white flowers. And they're all attractive.

Each plant has an illustration and brief description to help you recognize it and determine if it's right for you. Basic care symbols illustrate how much effort a plant requires, while other symbols show how much water and light it needs.

## BASIC CARE SYMBOLS

 <u>Very Easy Care</u>. If you want a plant that you can almost ignore, look for this symbol.

 <u>Easy Care</u>. If you can give a plant some water occasionally, try one with this symbol.

 <u>Light Active Care</u>. If you can pay regular attention to a plant, check out this symbol.

 <u>Active Care</u>. If you're willing to shoulder a lot of plant responsibility, try a plant with this symbol.

## WATER SYMBOLS

 <u>Moderate</u>. The top inch of soil will be dry for a day or two. Weekly watering should be fine.

 <u>Wet</u>. The soil should be kept consistently moist. Water at least weekly and check every few days. Give a light watering if the soil surface feels dry.

# LIGHT SYMBOLS

 __Moderate Light__. This would be some distance away from east, west or south windows, or closer if curtains filter the light. You could cast a dim shadow on plants in moderate light.

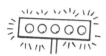 __Bright Light__. But not necessarily full sun. These conditions are found close to east, west and south windows, and there may be times when the area gets direct sunlight. For plants that don't like full sun, put up a filtering shade or move the plant out of the sun's path.

Some flowering plants will bloom repeatedly, but others are bred to be one-shot wonders. You could jump through 27 hoops to get the plant to bloom again, but it's best to thank the plant for its performance and then toss it when the show's over. So you don't knock yourself out trying to get a short-timer plant to bloom again, look for Plant Duration Symbols.

Use the symbols to help you decide which plants to try. If you're lacking a meaningful relationship in your life, try a plant that needs babying. If you just want a brief burst of color to keep you cheerful while your in-laws are visiting, buy a short-timer plant, and hope the relatives don't stick around longer than the blossoms. Because flowering plants are sold in bloom, some are only available at certain times of the year. I'll tell you when.

## PLANT DURATION SYMBOLS

 <u>Short-timer</u>. Discard the plant after blooms have died.

 <u>Long-timer</u>. Follow individual plant instructions in this book to encourage further blooming.

This book also has tips on feeding each plant and treating pests or diseases that may afflict your plants. Additional information on these and other topics begins on page 51, **More About Plant Care**. But now, put on your shades and meet the bright and beautiful Bloomin' Bunch!

# CHRYSANTHEMUMS

 Easy Care

 Wet

 Bright

 Short-Timer

The Chrysanthemum is an attractive, traditional plant. Long-lasting flowers come in many different colors. Watch for aphids and leaf miners. Available all year.

Where I come from in New England, it's an unwritten law that you have to put a Chrysanthemum next to the pumpkin on your front porch in the fall. It never fails; one day you're frolicking at the beach, the next the tanning oil is packed away and you're putting 'Mums out. This autumn ritual provides a final bit of flowering color outdoors before the long winter sets in, but you can buy these plants all year 'round.

Known as *Florist* or *Pot Chrysanthemums*, these are sturdy plants with a somewhat reserved character. They're lovely without being flashy. Most plants are no more than a foot tall. The many-lobed leaves are a dark, smoky green and grow to several inches long on tough green stems. 'Mum blossoms can be white, pink, mauve, rust, yellow — almost every color but blue — and come in many different forms. Some flowers are like daisies, with a single row of simple petals around a yellow center. Others have many rows of ruffled petals that obscure the center. Button 'Mums have smaller blooms, with almost tubular petals forming a half-dome shape.

'Mums have a distinctive scent that some might call bitter. For me the smell brings back memories of jumping in a pile of golden leaves on an October afternoon. With proper care, 'Mum flowers should last about six weeks. It's difficult to get them to bloom a second time, so discard them after they've finished flowering. If you like them, you can always buy more. You can even try different colors to match the seasons.

Some people plant their 'Mums outside after the blooms have faded. Most Pot Chrysanthemums have been specially developed to grow indoors, and are quite different from the hardy perennial varieties that survive harsh winters and bloom in the autumn garden. But you can always give it a try. There's no harm done if the plant doesn't make it.

## Light Requirements for Chrysanthemums

Put this plant in bright light or in a sunny window that's filtered by a curtain.

## Watering Chrysanthemums

Water every five to seven days, and pour off any water remaining in the drainage saucer after 20 minutes. Check the soil periodically with your finger to make sure it's fairly moist. Don't let the soil dry out.

## Temperature Requirements for Chrysanthemums

'Mums prefer cooler temperatures, preferably below 68° during the day and below 55° at night. In warmer rooms, blossoms won't last as long.

## Feeding Chrysanthemums

This short-timer plant will hold its blooms without fertilizer.

## Trimming and Cleaning Chrysanthemums

To keep 'Mums looking their best, remove blossoms as they fade. Also remove yellowing leaves.

## Pests, Diseases and Chrysanthemums

This plant is vulnerable to aphids and leaf miners, but resistant to disease. Remove aphids by hand or use a contact insecticide. Pick off leaves damaged by leaf miners and treat plant with contact or systemic insecticide. See page 74 for more about pests and pest control.

For more about all of these subjects, see page 51, **More About Plant Care.**

## RIEGER BEGONIA

   Easy Care

   Moderate

   Bright, Some Sun

   Short-Timer

The Rieger Begonia is a rich-looking plant that will brighten up a winter home. Dark foliage contrasts beautifully with the bright flowers. Watch for mildew. Commonly available in the spring, but can be found all year.

Break out the cappuccino and Linzer Torte when you bring home a Rieger Begonia. These plants are fairly new hybrids that have recently been introduced into the States from Europe. If you're familiar with the common *Wax Begonia* that's a staple in summer gardens, consider these winter-blooming plants to be their wealthy and classy cousins.

The two- to three-inch-wide flower blossoms have several layers of papery petals and grow in clusters. The blossoms come in vibrant shades of red, pink, rose, orange or yellow. Rieger Begonias grow up to eighteen inches tall on dark red stems. The glossy, round leaves are a deep green and grow to three inches across.

Rieger Begonias are available in flower during the winter. The rich, colorful blossoms will last for months, but it's difficult to get them to bloom again. Once the show's over, discard the plant and look forward to welcoming some new European visitors the next winter.

## Light Requirements for the Rieger Begonia

Provide at least four hours of sun a day during winter. If the plant is still blooming in March, move it to bright light away from direct sun.

## Watering the Rieger Begonia

Water once a week and let the soil become a bit dry between waterings. Pour off any excess drainage water after 20 minutes. Avoid overwatering, which can lead to mildew.

## Temperature Requirements for the Rieger Begonia

These plants like average day temperatures of 68° to 72°, and fairly cool nights between 50° and 60°.

## Feeding the Rieger Begonia

Fertilize plants every two weeks, and never use more fertilizer than recommended on the package. For more about plant food, see page 60.

## Trimming and Cleaning the Rieger Begonia

Remove blooms as they fade to keep the plant looking good. Cut any yellowing, unhealthy or unattractive leaves back to a main stem. If the leaves get dusty, wipe them with a damp sponge.

## Pests, Diseases and the Rieger Begonia

This plant is resistant to most pests, but can be vulnerable to mildew. Remove leaves affected by mildew and treat the plant with a fungicide. See page 77 and 78 for more information.

For more about all of these subjects, turn to page 51, **More About Plant Care.**

# KALANCHOE

 Very Easy Care

 Moderate

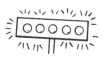 Bright, Some Sun

 Short-Timer

This plant provides a bit of whimsy during the winter months. Small blossoms have intense color. Watch for mealy bugs. Available all year.

There's no better way to describe a Kalanchoe than "cute." Its compact size and perky little flowers hovering on tall stems make me think of gnomes and butterflies and rambling little forest paths. I'm sure Dorothy skipped past a few on her way down the Yellow Brick Road. These winter-flowering plants are sure to brighten your home with their sunny disposition.

The Kalanchoe is a succulent, and has the thick, fleshy leaves common to many plants of this type. (Cacti are succulents, in case you were wondering.) The waxy, round leaves grow one to two inches long and have little notches and red coloring along the edges. Without flowers, a Kalanchoe would seem pretty macho; the leaves look like they could scrape paint. Ahh... but then the flowers soar above the leaves like tiny fireworks.

Kalanchoe blossoms are small, no more than a half-inch across with four small petals, but they grow in tightly packed heads having 20 to 50 flowers each. The flower heads look like little bouquets on stalks that reach eight to ten inches tall. The blossoms come in shades of red, orange, gold, pink and coral and will last up to three months.

Kalanchoes can grow to fifteen inches tall; a dwarf variety reaches eight inches. It's possible to force a second bloom, but it's better

to leave that task to the nursery. Treat yourself to new Kalanchoes as winter approaches.

## Light Requirements for the Kalanchoe

Give Kalanchoes a bright spot, with at
least four hours of direct sun each day.

## Watering the Kalanchoe

Water once every seven to ten days, letting the soil become nearly dry between waterings. Pour off any excess water from the
drainage saucer after 20 minutes.

## Temperature Requirements for the Kalanchoe

The Kalanchoe prefers day temperatures
of 68° to 72° and night temperatures between
50° and 60°.

## Feeding the Kalanchoe

Feed once a month while the plant is
flowering. Never use more fertilizer than the
package recommends. Check page 60 for
more about fertilizer.

## Trimming and Cleaning the Kalanchoe

Remove flowers as they fade, and cut off
the stalk of a completely faded flower head
at its base. Wipe dusty leaves with a damp
sponge.

### Pests, Diseases and the Kalanchoe

Kalanchoes are susceptible to mealy bugs. Use insecticide to control them. Page 74 introduces more about pests and pest control.

For more about all of these subjects, turn to page 51, **More About Plant Care.**

# BROMELIADS

Light Active Care

Wet

Moderate to Bright

Long-Timer

Bromeliads are striking plants that are available in many varieties. Leaves and flower stalks provide long-lasting color. Special watering and feeding techniques are required. Available all year.

Striking, different, remarkable, beautiful. With a name like *Bromeliad,* you might expect something out of a horticultural science fiction flick, and you wouldn't be far off. These plants are related to pineapples, and if you've ever felt the leafy top of a pineapple you have an idea of what these plants are like. Bromeliads are easy to grow and provide long-lasting color. Get ready; these plants are very different.

There are many different varieties of Bromeliads, enough so that some people collect them. Some have fairly short and flat profiles, while others grow taller with sweeping leaves. All types have leaves that grow in a rosette, or cluster, from the soil. Many of these plants grow in the wild on trees, without soil. The leaves have developed scales that absorb water and nutrients, and these often appear as striped markings on the leaves. The center cup of the plant rosette also holds water.

While Bromeliads can flower at any time, the blossoms themselves are usually uninspiring. It's what the plant does when flowering that makes it colorful and impressive.

Two of the shorter varieties are the *Blushing Bromeliad* and the *Bird's Nest Bromeliad.* These have strap-like leaves two to three inches wide and up to ten inches long. The

Blushing Bromeliad has light green leaves striped with ivory, while the Bird's Nest has solid, dark green leaves. Just before blooming, the center leaves blush with pink, purple or dark red. Small purple or white flowers will bloom in the center cup for a short time, but the leaves will keep their rich color for months after the blossoms have faded.

Taller varieties include *Flaming Swords, Guzmanias* and *Tillandsias*. Flaming Swords have stiff, strap-like leaves often banded with silvery scales. They sweep upward to twelve inches and grow two to three inches wide. The red "sword" grows up from the center and can reach two to three feet tall. The sword is tightly covered in *bracts*, small red leaves that cup the flower blossoms. While the blossoms die quickly, the beautiful sword will last for months.

Guzmanias have softer, upward-sweeping leaves that are light green and reach twelve inches in length. They send up a central stalk that bears small white flowers for a brief time in winter. After the blossoms fade, red and yellow bracts appear, sweeping outward like a miniature, colored version of the main plant and lasting for weeks.

Tillandsias have long, narrow, pointed leaves ranging from lemony green to gray-green and reaching six to eight inches. From fall through spring a wide, flat spike tightly covered in pinkish bracts appears in the center. The spike can reach eight to ten inches tall. Blue, fragrant flowers appear one at a time on the spike.

These plants are available any time of year and are usually sold just before they flower. Bromeliads tend to die after flowering, but they do send out little offshoots that can be separated and grown into mature plants. See page 73 for more information. Bromeliads grow slowly and new plants can take years to flower. Repot them when the roots have filled the pot. Page 67 introduces tips about repotting.

## Light Requirements for Bromeliads

Depending on the variety, some Bromeliads can tolerate moderate light, while others need a few hours of direct sun each day. Bright indirect light or curtain-filtered sun is a safe bet for all Bromeliads, but check the care tag on the plant you buy.

## Watering Bromeliads

Water the soil once a week, letting it become a bit dry between waterings. Pour off any excess water from the drainage saucer after 20 minutes.

Bromeliads like to keep a little pitcher of water by the bed, so to speak. Since many of these plants grow on the sides of trees in the wild, they don't have true roots to take up water, so they've adapted by using the cup in the center of the rosette to hold rainwater. Even inside the house, they still like their cup to runneth nearly over. When watering Bromeliads, water the soil and leaves and keep the cup filled with water. About once a month, tip the plant upside down to drain the cup and refill it with fresh water. Bromeliads also enjoy extra humidity. See page 56 for more about humidity.

## Feeding Bromeliads

Fertilize Bromeliads monthly. Use liquid fertilizer solution prepared at half the strength recommended on the package. Pour the solution on the soil, over the leaves and into the rosette cup. It's best to use distilled water; water that contains lime can stain the leaves.

## Trimming and Cleaning Bromeliads

Remove faded blossoms from the central cup to keep them from rotting in the water. Blossoms that grow in bracts should fall away themselves. To trim leaves, use scissors and trim any browning or unhealthy sections, following the leaf's natural shape. To remove dust from the leaves, wipe them with a sponge moistened with distilled water.

## Pests, Diseases and Bromeliads

These plants are resistant to most pests and diseases.

For more information about these subjects, turn to page 51, **More About Plant Care.**

## INDOOR AZALEA

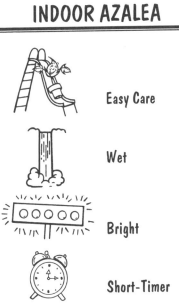

Easy Care

Wet

Bright

Short-Timer

The Indoor Azalea is a traditional shrub with brilliant color. Flowers only last a few weeks, but foliage is attractive. Needs moist soil and cool temperatures. Commonly available in the spring; can be found all year.

Azaleas make me think of the Kentucky Derby, sunny days, mosquitoes — in other words, springtime. The Azaleas we commonly see outdoors herald the arrival of warmer days with their billows of rich colors. With Indoor Azaleas, you can get that same giddy, spring-fever feeling beginning in November. They are a common gift plant for the winter and spring holidays.

The blossoms of Azalea shrubs are so bright you almost need to wear shades. The soft-petaled, one- to four-inch flowers grow in billowy masses of red, magenta, coral, pink or white. Some blossoms have two colors. The small, dark green leaves can be glossy or velvety, and grow on brown, woody stems covered in soft bristles. Azaleas reach anywhere from six inches to two feet tall, with a similar spread.

With proper care, blossoms will last from two to four weeks. Many people plant the Azalea outdoors after the flowers fade, and wonder why it doesn't become a lovely shrub, blooming year after year. There's a reason why this plant is called an *Indoor* Azalea; it's been developed to grow and bloom inside as a houseplant. Don't waste your time planting it out in the yard. Unfortunately, it's difficult to get the Indoor Azalea to bloom again inside. After the blooms have faded, discard the plant, or enjoy the nice foliage for awhile.

### Light Requirements for the Indoor Azalea

Showcase this plant in bright indirect light or curtain-filtered sun. Keep it out of direct sun, which will fade the flowers.

### Watering the Indoor Azalea

Water every five to seven days. Pour off any water remaining in the drainage saucer after 20 minutes. Check the soil with your finger every few days to make sure it's moist. If the soil dries out, the leaves will drop off.

### Temperature Requirements for the Indoor Azalea

Azaleas like cooler temperatures, 68° or lower during the day and 40° to 55° at night. Higher temperatures will shorten the life of the blossoms.

### Feeding the Indoor Azalea

This Azalea doesn't need fertilizer when it is flowering.

### Trimming and Cleaning the Indoor Azalea

To keep this plant looking great, use scissors to remove blossoms as they fade.

## Pests, Diseases and the Indoor Azalea

Azaleas are resistant to most pests and diseases.

For more information about these subjects, turn to page 51, **More About Plant Care.**

# AFRICAN VIOLETS

 Active Care

 Moderate

 Bright

 Long-Timer

African Violets are small, elegant and beautiful plants with a very traditional character. Will bloom continuously with the right care. Watch for mealy bugs and disease. Available all year.

Without a doubt, this is the most popular flowering houseplant in America. There are literally thousands of different varieties. African Violets have a good thing going for themselves. There's special African Violet fertilizer and African Violet soil. I guess when you're a beautiful star of the houseplant world and have a good PR person, you can get some of those perks. Next thing you know they'll have an athletic shoe contract.

African Violets have heart-shaped, hairy leaves about two to four inches long, growing in a flattened rosette on fleshy stems. The leaves range from bronze to dark green, and often have red undersides and stems. But the real draw is the flowers — velvety one- to two-inch blossoms that grow in clusters on thin stalks above the leaves. The flowers come in many different shades of blue, purple, pink and white. Some flowers are edged in a second color. Bright yellow stamens provide a striking accent to the petals. Blossoms can have a single row or many rows of petals, which can have smooth or ruffled edges. The plants will spread to about eight inches and reach four to six inches tall.

African Violets are available all year. If you take good care of them, they will bloom continuously. Repot them every two or three years in African Violet potting mixture, available at nurseries and garden shops. They prefer shallow pots, no bigger than four inches across. Bigger pots can lead to over-watering.

### Light Requirements for African Violets

These plants bloom best in bright indirect light or filtered sunlight. Keep them out of direct sunlight.

### Watering African Violets

Water once a week with tepid water, pouring off any water left in the drainage saucer after 20 minutes. Let the soil get slightly dry between waterings; African Violets are easily killed by overwatering. Be sure to water only the soil. Avoid wetting the leaves, which can cause brown leaf spots or gray mold. Water lodged in the central crown where the stalks meet can lead to disease. Consider watering plants from below, filling the drainage saucer with water and emptying any that's remaining after 30 minutes. These plants also enjoy extra humidity. Go to page 56 for tips.

## Temperature Requirements for African Violets

These delicate plants like it pretty toasty, with evening temperatures between 65° and 70°, and day temperatures 75° to 80°.

## Feeding African Violets

Use African Violet fertilizer prepared at one-quarter the recommended strength. Fertilize every time you water. Check page 60.

## Trimming and Cleaning African Violets

Remove blossoms as they fade. Cut yellow or unattractive leaves back to the base. Gently sweep dust and debris from leaves using a dry paintbrush with a flat edge.

## Pests, Diseases and African Violets

This plant is vulnerable to mealy bugs, gray mold and crown rot. Control mealy bugs with insecticide. For gray mold, remove affected leaves and avoid getting leaves wet. Use fungicide for severe cases. Crown rot is usually fatal; discard the plant to keep from infecting others. See page 74 for more information.

For more information about all of these subjects, turn to page 51, **More About Plant Care.**

# GLOXINIA

 Active Care

 Wet

 Bright

 Long-Timer

Large, deep green leaves and richly colored flowers make the Gloxinia a very attractive plant. Blooms any time of the year. Goes dormant for several months. Available mid-winter through spring.

I'm sure the Gloxinia can be found in the castles of every European royal. Maybe it's the velvety flowers' rich colors, which make me think of red carpets and ermine. Or maybe it's their trumpet shape. When I see Gloxinias, a little flourish of horns goes through my head, as if announcing the arrival of Her Majesty. Okay, I admit to a few delusions of grandeur. But if I can't have the castle, I can at least have the flower.

The Gloxinia has oval, velvety leaves that grow eight inches long by six inches wide on hairy, purplish stems. The leaves are dark green with pale green veins; the undersides are flushed with red. The flowers grow above the leaves on thin stems and can range from three to six inches across. Depending on the variety, flowers can have five petals or many more petals, some with ruffled edges. The rich colors include deep red, lavender, purple, pink and white. Some flowers are edged or spotted in a second color.

These plants are related to African Violets, and personally I think they're more attractive. But like all aristocrats, they are a bit particular. Gloxinias may blossom at any time, but will go completely dormant for several months. (The royals need their nap, don't you know.) Stop fertilizing them when the flowers fade, and gradually reduce watering. When the leaves wither, stop watering completely. In two to four months, new sprouts will appear. Repot the plant, start watering and fertilizing again, and prepare for another show of regal blossoms.

### Light Requirements for the Gloxinia
Put the Gloxinia in a spot that gets bright indirect or filtered light.

### Watering the Gloxinia
Water every five to seven days, and pour off any water left in the drainage saucer after 20 minutes. Don't let the soil dry out; it can cause flower buds to wilt and fall off. Check the soil with your finger every few days to make sure it's moist. Gloxinias like humid conditions. For tips, go to page 56.

### Temperature Requirements for the Gloxinia
The Gloxinia does best in warm conditions, 75° to 80° during the day and 65° to 70° at night.

### Feeding the Gloxinia
Fertilize once a month while the Gloxinia is growing; don't feed it when it's dormant. Never use more fertilizer than the package

recommends. For more information, see page 60.

### Trimming and Cleaning the Gloxinia

Remove flowers as they fade. Cut off yellow or unattractive leaves at their base. Use a soft, dry paintbrush to sweep the leaves clean. Cut away withered leaves on a dormant plant after it sprouts new leaves.

### Pests, Diseases and the Gloxinia

The Gloxinia is resistant to most pests and diseases.

For more information about these subjects, turn to page 51, **More About Plant Care.**

# CYCLAMEN

Active Care

Wet

Bright

Short-Timer

The Cyclamen is a pretty, winter-flowering plant with unique blossoms. Prefers very cool temperatures. Avoid overwatering. Watch for aphids and mites. Available mid-fall through early spring.

Cyclamens give the impression that you could wind them up and they'd fly around the room. Some people think the flowers look like butterflies. But, playing off of the plant's name, I think they look like mini cyclones. Picture walking into the middle of a whirlwind with wet hair and standing there until it dries, and you'll get an idea of what a Cyclamen's petals are like.

This plant has firm, heart-shaped leaves growing on fleshy stems. The leaves are dark green with silvery markings, and can grow to several inches across. The two- to three-inch flowers spring above the leaves on fleshy stalks. Depending on the variety, the petals can be pink, salmon, red or white and are swept back from the center, as if the flowers are turned inside out. The cool green leaves and sweet-colored petals give an overall effect of cotton candy. With their winged, whirling blossoms, Cyclamens can reach a foot in height.

The Cyclamen is a popular winter holiday gift plant. It will bloom continuously for months as long as the temperature is fairly cool. Higher temperatures will shorten the blooming period and keep young flower buds from opening. It's difficult to get this plant to bloom again, so discard it when the last of the flowers has faded.

## Light Requirements for the Cyclamen

This plant does best in filtered sun or bright indirect light. It can tolerate a few hours of direct winter sun.

## Watering the Cyclamen

Water every five to seven days and pour off any water left in the drainage saucer after 20 minutes. Check with your finger every few days to make sure the soil is moist. Never let the Cyclamen wilt, as it usually doesn't recover. The Cyclamen has a bulbous central root that's like a turnip. I steer clear of this vegetable, and it's a good idea to keep your distance from this root when you're watering. If it gets too wet, it can begin to rot. Pour water around the rim of a Cyclamen's pot to avoid showering the fat bulb. Or consider watering from the bottom by filling a deep drainage saucer with water and emptying any water left after 30 minutes.

## Temperature Requirements for the Cyclamen

This plant flourishes at cooler temperatures, 65° or lower during the day and 40° to 55° at night.

## Feeding the Cyclamen

Fertilize the Cyclamen every two weeks.

Never use more fertilizer than the manufacturer recommends. See page 60 for more tips.

### Trimming and Cleaning the Cyclamen

Cut faded blossoms and yellowing or unattractive leaves back to the base of the plant.

### Pinching and Pruning the Cyclamen

Because leaves and flowers grow up from the soil, the Cyclamen doesn't require pinching or pruning.

### Pests, Diseases and the Cyclamen

This plant is vulnerable to aphids and cyclamen mites. Remove aphids by hand or use insecticide. Use insecticide to kill mites, or discard infected plants. See page 74 for more about pests and pest control.

For more information about all of these subjects, turn to page 51, **More About Plant Care.**

# HOW TO CHOOSE
# A FLOWERING HOUSEPLANT

**Decisions, Decisions...**

When shopping for a flowering house-plant, you'll be faced with a lot of decisions. These aren't just off-the-cuff decisions you can make willy-nilly. The choices you make can mean the difference between horticultural heaven or a flowering fiasco. These are life and death decisions — for the plant, that is.

If you're looking for a flowering plant, then you've already made one determination: you want flowers. But before you skip merrily off to the nursery, there are other points you need to consider.

Does your house get enough light? Most flowering plants need fairly bright light to keep the blossoms going. If your place has the cheery brightness of a gothic castle, you may want to think twice about getting a Kalanchoe or Gloxinia. About the only flowering plants that can tolerate less light, but still need moderate light, are Bromeliads.

Second point: Is this the right time for you to muster up the effort and discipline to keep a plant's soil moist? Are you going to be away traveling, or working long hours on a project, or otherwise totally occupied? Many flowering plants need consistent moisture. If you've got the time, it's a small price to pay for beautiful blooms. But if you're too busy, you might be better off getting a foliage plant, and waiting to purchase a flowering houseplant when you are better able to take care of it.

The key to growing any houseplant successfully is really nothing more than providing the right growing conditions. Many foliage plants will thrive under conditions that would make a flowering plant miserable. But even if you don't have the right conditions, it's not written in stone that you be deprived of colorful blossoms. You just may want to purchase plants that have a shorter life span, and understand that their blooming show may be cut even shorter by your dark and dry household. Which leads us to our next decision point.

## Brief Tryst or Lifelong Commitment?

Flowering plants are performers. Most put on a razzle-dazzle display of color, and then take a nap when the show's over. Sometimes they take a long nap. Sometimes they won't bloom again unless you give them special care and play mind games to force them to flower. I say, leave this to the nurseries. It's too much effort and we've all got better things to do than making a Chrysanthemum think it's October in the middle of March. Besides, most flowering plants look about as attractive as we do when we're napping, and who wants something like that hanging around for months?

When you're sure that you want a flowering plant and have the right conditions to keep it happy, decide if you want a plant that will put down some roots in your house or a plant that will entertain for a few weeks until the circus rolls out of town again.

The plant descriptions in this book identify plants that are short-timers and long-timers. If you want continuous blooms to brighten your boudoir, buy an African Violet. The other long-lasting plants are Bromeliads and Gloxinias, and even these have their dormant periods. Actually, Bromeliads die after they bloom, which I guess is the ultimate in dormancy. But they do send out baby plants to keep up the show.

The rest of the Bloomin' Bunch are short-timers. Like most other things, "short" is a relative term. With proper care, Azalea blooms will last two to four weeks, while a Kalanchoe or Cyclamen will bloom for months. But no matter how long the show lasts, when it's over just throw the plant in the trash. Wash and save the pot for other plants; there's no reason to be wasteful. And don't feel bad; many expensive Broadway shows have closed after one night.

If you're okay with the concept of short-timer plants, and won't have trouble throwing one away, be aware of their blooming seasons. True, red Gloxinias may be glorious for the Fourth of July, but they're not available in mid-summer. Flowering plants determine when you can decorate with them, not the other way around. This book indicates each plant's blooming season, which is when they are usually available for sale. (You can avoid looking silly asking, "Where are the Cyclamens?" in a garden shop in May.)

## A Hundred and One Flavors

Let's face it, we buy flowering plants for the color, not for green leaves. Picking a color is the last decision you need to make, and it's obviously the most fun. The blossoms of flowering plants can be white, yellow, gold, red, orange, pink, magenta, purple, blue, salmon — get the picture? Choose a color that matches the room where it will be staying, or just pick a color that makes you feel good!

---

### THE FLOWERING HOUSEPLANT SHOPPER'S CHECKLIST

1. Do I want a flowering plant?
2. Do I have enough light for a flowering plant?
3. Can I keep a flowering plant moist?
4. Do I want a long-timer or short-timer plant?
5. If I want a short-timer plant, what's the blooming season?
6. What color blooms do I want?

---

Foliage plants last for a long time, but flowering plants are special treats. Buying one is like taking yourself out for an ice cream (and the plant should last longer). So if you're in a silly Peppermint Stick mood, buy yourself a pink Cyclamen. Prefer traditional French Vanilla? Get a cool white Azalea. Want some decadent Blueberry Cheesecake? Buy a royal blue Gloxinia.

## Now for Some Technical Stuff

Once you've made all of your decisions and settled on a plant that's right for you, buy one that's healthy and attractive. This isn't much different from shopping for produce. Do you buy yellow, wilted lettuce? Probably not. Do you buy unripe cantaloupe? (And if you can tell when one's ripe, please explain it to me.)

Avoid plants with wilted or yellow leaves or straggly stems. Look for plants that have a nice shape, are evenly covered with leaves and have plenty of blossoms and buds. Be sure at least half of the buds are open. It may seem like a good idea to buy a plant with closed buds so you'll get to enjoy every blossom at home, but without the right conditions, the buds may never open. This is especially true of Chrysanthemums. (Remember, you're buying a flowering plant, not a foliage plant with flower buds.) In the end, choose a plant that looks good. That should be easy.

There are a few other tricks to buying quality plants. Make sure the soil feels moist and fairly loose in the pot. If it feels dry, hard or is covered in mossy mildew, move on. Check for signs of pests and disease too. Look at the leaves and stalks for mold, mushy brown spots or bugs. Even if you're only buying a short-timer plant, you don't want to spend the time nursing it. And you might risk infecting your other plants. See page 74 to learn the specific signs of pests and diseases that might affect the Bloomin' Bunch.

Finally, if the plants in a store don't seem healthy or well cared for, take your business elsewhere.

## You'll Spend a Few Bucks for Beautiful Blossoms

Flowering plants cost a little more than foliage plants. Nurseries work hard to get a plant to flower, so that you and your friends "ooh" and "ahh" when you bring it home. You can pay anywhere from $4.99 for a small African Violet at a discount store to $25 for an Azalea at a florist.

## ISOLATE A NEW PLANT

Even if you've checked, you still might bring a sick plant home. Pests lick their chops when they're close to a new healthy plant; they just climb aboard and start munching. So keep any new plant away from other plants for a few weeks. Flowering plants are special and deserve their own spotlight anyway. If, after a few weeks, the plant still looks healthy, you can move it closer to other plants. Don't worry if a few lower leaves turn yellow and die. This is just the plant adjusting to a new place and shedding a few tears over its old one.

The rule for buying a plant is the same as for buying a car or a suit or a lamb chop — get the highest quality at the lowest price. Because it is fairly easy to see the quality of a flowering plant, and because the same nurseries supply garden stores and grocery stores and all manner of stores, with a discriminating eye you are likely to get a healthy plant in any number of places. Many flowering houseplants are connected with holidays and gift-giving. Pay attention to the capitalist mantra of supply and demand, too! Three days before Thanksgiving, a pot of 'Mums is going to cost big bucks, and when you're eating the last turkey sandwich on Monday, the same plant will be a lot cheaper.

## SAVE THE FOIL FOR THE TURKEY

Because flowering plants are popular for holidays or as presents, many are packaged for gift-giving. Their pots may be wrapped in shiny foil, or plastic printed with bunnies or Santas or lovely sentiments. This might look pretty, but it doesn't let water drain out of the pot. While that elf on the paper may be happy, the plant could be drowning. Remove the paper and put the pot in a proper drainage saucer or another attractive container. Or if you want to keep the paper on during a long holiday season, cut some holes in it and put the pot on a saucer. This will allow water to drain and the foil to sparkle with holiday cheer.

# MORE ABOUT PLANT CARE

## Water

### Take a Bow, Take a Drink

Right after athletes or dancers put on an impressive performance, what do they do? They take a drink of water to replenish their bodies. It clears toxins and helps the blood flow with oxygen and nutrients. The Bloomin' Bunch exert a lot of effort to flower, and they need lots of water to stay healthy and attractive.

Water is like a plant's blood, carrying nutrients from root tip to flower petal. If we had too much — or too little — blood in our bodies, we wouldn't be doing very well. The same is true of houseplants and water. Not enough water can make a plant spindly and cause blossoms to fall off. Too much can cause a plant to rot. Most flowering plants prefer moist conditions, so you need to watch for signs of underwatering. Then again, some of the fleshier plants are just a few sips away from turning into mush. So check the tips on how and when to water plants, and pay attention to the special needs of some flowering plants.

## How to Water

After you've mowed the lawn on a steamy day or bounced around an aerobics class for an hour, do you take just a few sips of water? No! You suck down a glass or two because you're thirsty! Now imagine if you were a plant and only got a drink about once a week.

## WORDS FOR THE WATER-WISE

- Growth slows.
- Leaves wilt or become limp.
- Lower leaves curl, yellow or fall off.
- Leaf edges turn brown and dry.
- Flowers fade and fall off quickly.

- Leaves get soft, rotten patches.
- Leaves curl, yellow and tips turn brown.
- Young and old leaves fall off.
- Leaf growth is poor.
- Flowers turn moldy.

You may like to think of your flowering plants as delicate beauties who have weak tea and watercress sandwiches on Saturday afternoons. But as lovely as these plants may be, they drink like a laborer who's been laying track in the desert all day. Give your plants a full, satisfying drink each time you water them. Don't just dribble a few drops on the soil; the roots need to take up enough water for the whole plant. Pour water all around the soil until it comes out of the pot's drainage holes. Make sure there's a saucer underneath to catch the drainage. Believe me, you don't want to learn this lesson the hard way.

After 20 minutes, check the drainage saucer and dump out any water that's left. By this time, the soil and roots have absorbed as much as they can, and any remaining water can cause problems.

## Some Special Watering Tips

Most of the Bloomin' Bunch will do fine with your basic pour-water-on-the-soil technique. But a few of them have special needs; be sure to check the special instructions that follow each plant description in the **Flowering Houseplants** chapter.

For some plants, including both Cyclamens and African Violets, you can also water from the bottom. Rather than pouring water onto the soil and letting it drain out, pour water into a deep drainage saucer and let the soil and roots suck up the water. This should take about 30 minutes. After that, pour any remaining water out; these guys will keep drinking until they rot! If you do use this method consistently, water the plant occasionally from the top to flush out any accumulated fertilizer that may build up in the soil. (See page 62 for more on this topic.)

## When to Water

Basically, you water a plant when it needs water. To tell if a plant needs water, use the ultra-scientific *Finger Test*. Developed after years of research under a massive federal grant program, this complex test has been proven accurate 99.97 percent of the time. To conduct the test, stick a dry finger, preferably your own, into the soil about an inch. If the soil feels dry, it needs water. For flowering plants that like very moist conditions, use the finger to feel the top of the soil. If it feels moist, the plant is okay.

A second method, known as the *Finger and Eye Test,* requires examination of the plant itself. If the leaves feel limp or look droopy, research has shown that the plant needs water. If the leaves feel crunchy and look brown, all research points to a dead plant. Unfortunately, no amount of water can revive the dead.

Even though flowering plants like moist conditions, moderation is the best approach. It's always better to underwater than over-water, so if you're not sure, wait another day or so.

## WHAT'S ON THE WATER MENU?

Years ago we all drank water from the tap. Now it seems we have to drink bottled water from primordial springs and ancient glaciers. Isn't marketing wonderful? What comes out of the tap is fine for watering most plants. Water that smells or tastes of chlorine should be set in an open container overnight to let the chlorine evaporate. Water softeners use chemicals that can damage plants, so it's a good idea to use cheap, gallon-jug bottled water instead. Bromeliad leaves can stain from lime in tap water. Keep a bottled of distilled water on hand for these picky plants. (There's always one in the crowd, isn't there?) Whatever type of water you use, make sure it feels pleasantly warm; cold water can shock plants.

## CAN YOU SAY, "MOIST?"

Flowering plants like their soil to be moist, not wet. What's the difference? Try this simple test. When you're in the shower, wash one side of your head with the leading dandruff shampoo... wait a minute, that's a different test. When you get out of the shower, feel your hair before drying it. As long as you don't have a crew cut, your hair should be saturated with water. This is commonly known as "wet." Lightly towel dry your hair and feel it again. It should feel cool and damp. This condition is known as "moist." This is how a plant's soil should feel. If the soil is wet and muddy, oxygen can't get to the roots and the plant will drown. Remember: moist, never wet!

## Humidity

### Not Everyone Hates Humidity

In some parts of the U.S., people always gripe during the muggy summer about the unbearable humidity. But many of the Bloomin' Bunch prefer high humidity; they'd be singing a happy tune on those days when you feel like you're walking and breathing in pea soup.

For foliage houseplants, the easiest way to increase humidity is with mist. But this heavy moisture on leaves and blossoms can cause rot and disease, so avoid misting flowering

plants. Your best option is to set plants on shallow trays filled with pebbles and water. The water will evaporate and create a little private steam room for the plant.

When you take a shower in the bathroom or boil water in the kitchen, these rooms fill up with moisture. Bring your flowering plants in for a humidity treatment, but remember that the kitchen or bathroom may be too warm as permanent homes for these plants. If you want to go all out, get a room humidifier. It may seem extravagant for a plant, but in those dry winter months when your nose and throat feel like sandpaper, you'll gain a new appreciation for humidity.

# Light

## Finding Food from Above

Picture this: You're hiking with a friend. Your stomach is growling, and you reach in your backpack and discover with dismay that your so-called friend has left the trail mix in the car. Not to worry; you look up into the sun with your arms outstretched, and your body turns the sun's rays into carbohydrates. You've manufactured food from sunlight, and you're ready to carry on with the hike.

Obviously, people can't do this, but plants can. It's called photosynthesis. For plants, light is an essential food source. And the more

---

### THE DARK SIDE OF BRIGHT SPACES

Flowering plants do appreciate bright light, but be careful if you put them in a window. If the leaves or blossoms touch the glass, the hot summer sun or cold winter temperatures can hurt them. Even if they aren't touching the glass, plants on a windowsill can be shocked by cold winter drafts. Other plants such as Cyclamens that prefer very cool temperatures may enjoy the cooler space, so long as it doesn't get below 45°. Check your plant's light and temperature needs before putting it in a sunny window. The results may be less than sunny.

---

## HAVE A BITE OF SUNSHINE

The right condition for flowering plants is near a south-, east- or west-facing window. If you lived in a big, round house with a window in each direction, the bright part of this pie would be where you could grow one of the Bloomin' Bunch. If your house isn't round, your bright-light area might not look like pieces of pie, but you get the idea... keep the plants away from that dark area and those dark corners!

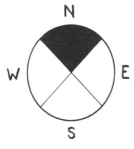

work a plant does, the more food it needs, which is why most flowering plants need bright light. It takes a lot of effort to develop gorgeous blooms!

Unless you live in a greenhouse, providing enough light for a plant depends on how much comes into a room from the windows. So it's important to find the right spot for your plant. For flowering plants, the best location would be near a south-, east- or west-facing window. If a particular plant doesn't like direct sun, make sure the light is filtered by a curtain or move the plant out of the sun's path. You wouldn't want those vibrant magenta blooms to fade to run-of-the-mill pink, would you?

Because plants need light, they grow toward it. Turn your plants occasionally to help them grow evenly. They don't need to be like Waltzing Matilda; just a quarter- or half-turn every few days or once a week will do. It depends on how quickly the plant grows. If the plant is leaning over like the Tower of Pisa, you've waited too long.

## Fertilizer

### Snack Time!

I'll always remember how good those three cookies and that small cup of orange juice tasted in kindergarten. After wolfing those down, I was ready to run around aimlessly for another hour or two. Even now, there's nothing like a snack to get your energy level back up. Whether it's an apple, a chocolate bar or a rice cake, those extra nutrients help you make it through a long day. Well, the rice cake will help you make it through the next five minutes, but just about any other food will give you a lift.

Even though plants could survive on a basic diet of water and light, they also benefit from a little snack. The added nutrients in fertilizer give flowering plants the energy boost they need to put out those beautiful blooms.

People need nutrients like Vitamin C, iron and calcium; houseplants need nitrogen (for active growth), phosphate (for strong roots) and potassium (for healthy leaves and flowers). The best general fertilizer for plants has a balanced blend of these minerals, listed on the package by three identical numbers such as 10-10-10. Fertilizer for flowering plants is also available. This has less nitrogen, to help the plant produce more flowers. The number representing nitrogen on the package would be lower, such as 0-10-10. (The package would probably also say in big letters, "FOR FLOWERING HOUSEPLANTS," so don't worry too much about the number scheme.) There's also special African Violet fertilizer available. If you're going to grow these plants, it's best to give them what they like to eat.

Houseplant food is available in liquids, powders, fish emulsion and time-release pellets or sticks. With liquid and powdered fertilizer, you mix some into the water

## DID YOU FLUSH?

If you fertilize plants regularly, you may need to clean the soil of accumulated salts. If you see a crumbly white crust on the soil, that's minerals that have turned to salts. Remove the crust with a spoon, and then flush the plant. No, this doesn't mean putting it down the toilet. Run a large amount of water through the soil and let it drain out to rinse away any salts. If the pot would hold a quart, then use two quarts of water to flush it. Plants that are fed regularly, and particularly plants that are watered from the bottom, should be flushed every few months.

for your plants. You do the same with fish emulsion, a good natural fertilizer that is what it sounds like, and smells just as bad. The time-release fertilizers are put into the soil and release nutrients each time you water. These will last up to several months. Because many of the Bloomin' Bunch are short-timers, and most prefer fairly frequent snacks, it's best to use the liquid, powder or fish emulsion varieties intended for flowering plants.

### Beware the Snack Attack

How many of you have started snacking — just a few chips before dinner — and then suddenly realized you've eaten the whole bag? Why am I the only one with my hand up?

You know how it is. You feel full, maybe a little guilty. The same thing can happen with feeding plants, only they won't feel guilty, you probably will.

To avoid overfeeding your plants, read the instructions on the fertilizer package and never use more food than recommended. In fact, it's better to use a little less, perhaps one-quarter to one-half less. Mix weaker fertilizer solutions, and don't feed more often than recommended in this book's plant descriptions.

## Trimming and Cleaning

### After the Bloom Fades

It is sad that most of the Bloomin' Bunch don't hang around forever. But there is one benefit: you don't have to worry about maintenance! Foliage plants that live in your house for years (hopefully) need their leaves trimmed and occasional showers or sponge baths to clean off household dust. Many flowering plants aren't in your house long enough to get dusty, and if the leaves are yellow, just pick 'em off.

With all blooming plants, even the short-timers, remove faded blossoms to keep them looking great. A Chrysanthemum with a dozen purple flowers will look a heck of a lot better without those three brown, withered blossoms. For softer plants like Gloxinias and Cyclamens, use your fingernails to pinch off faded flowers. For Azaleas, 'Mums and other tough-stemmed plants, use scissors.

Try not to leave a visible gaping wound where the flower was removed. 'Mums and  Azaleas have lots of leaves, so you can cut just below the faded blossom and it shouldn't be noticeable. But if you did this on a plant like a Kalanchoe, that sends flowers up on their own stalks, you'd have a bare stalk sticking up like an antenna. For these plants, cut the stalk at its base once the flower has faded. Make sure you don't cheat yourself of blooms, though. You may need to carefully snip a faded blossom or two off an African Violet or Kalanchoe stalk that still has some unopened buds. Once the stalk has bloomed its last bloom, hack it off.

### Extra Care for Long-Timers

Plants that hang around the house a little longer may need more than just a little de-flowering. If a few leaves become unhealthy or unattractive, they may need to be trimmed or removed. You also may need to remove dust from the leaves, which is not only unattractive, but can make it hard for the plant to breathe. (Yes, plants need air too!)

Trimming and cleaning isn't just cosmetic maintenance, it helps keep plants healthy and more resistant to pests and disease. Which is not something you can say for that $30 manicure.

## Trimming

Leaves that are withering or have brown tips or edges don't necessarily mean a plant is sick. Some may be weak or old. Or maybe the plant got shocked from a draft or the air is too dry. Removing those bits of brown and yellow can do wonders for a plant.

For short-timer plants that only bloom for a few weeks, just remove any leaves in poor condition. For short-timers like Kalanchoes that stick around a while, or for long-timers like African Violets and Bromeliads, you may want to trim the leaves. Use a pair of sharp scissors — and drum up any memories you have from arts and crafts class at summer camp. You need to trim leaves so they retain their natural shape; a round leaf with a flat-top cut just won't make the grade. Trim off any browning sections, and remove just enough healthy leaf if necessary to make it look even and natural. The trimmed leaf should look like a smaller version of the original.

On all plants, withered and yellowing leaves are weak and should be removed to keep the plant strong. When removing leaves, cut them back to the branch or base of the plant.

## Cleaning

Unless you live on a busy, dusty city street (like I do), most of your short-timer plants shouldn't be around long enough to need cleaning.

With foliage houseplants, there are two basic cleaning options: wiping leaves with a damp sponge or giving the plants a shower, either in the tub or with a kitchen sink sprayer. Flowering plants are a bit trickier; some leaves don't like to have their faces wiped, and some flowers can be damaged by showers. So let's look at the Bloomin' Bunch's cleaning needs. Remember, these are stars of the houseplant world; they deserve a little pampering.

First, 'Mums and Azaleas. They don't last long enough to need cleaning, and don't really show dust anyway. No Saturday night baths for these guys.

Kalanchoes are pretty sturdy, and can tolerate a gentle lukewarm shower. You can also wipe the leaves with a damp sponge. Rieger Begonias and Cyclamens shouldn't get too wet, so sponge their leaves rather than showering them.

Bromeliads are long-timers, with plenty of potential to get dusty leaves. Many of these plants are so tough you could probably clean the leaves with a power sander and they wouldn't even flinch. But just use a sponge dampened with distilled water; the lime in tap water can stain the leaves.

African Violets and Gloxinias need the most pampering. Their hairy leaves easily catch dust, but also hold surface water, which can cause spotting, mold and rot. For these plants, get a one-inch, flat-edged paintbrush with soft bristles. Use the brush to sweep dust and debris off the leaves. This can be a bit time-consuming, so pretend you're a little elfin sprite whose morning chore is to sweep the flowers clean for the day. Or just zone out and get it over with — whatever works.

## Repotting

### Just a Little Breathing Room

Moving a plant into another, usually larger, pot gives the plant nutrients from fresh soil and space to let the roots grow.

You only need to repot a few of the Bloomin' Bunch: African Violets, Bromeliads and Gloxinias. You can tell a plant needs re-potting if the soil dries out more quickly than usual between waterings. Repot African Violets about every two years. For Bromeliads, wait until the roots have filled the pot. If you see thick roots, through the pot's drainage holes, it's time. It's best to repot a plant in the early spring. The plant will use the extra nutrients and space to start a season of healthy growth. Gloxinias need to be repot-ted after they've awakened from their dor-mant state. This can happen at any time of the year, depending on when they began their nap.

## Pots and Soil

Choose a new pot that's about one to two inches wider at the top, and make sure the pot has drainage holes on the bottom. With-out holes for water to drain, it's much easier to overwater plants. African Violets should never be in a pot larger than four inches across; the extra soil can lead to overwatering.

Speaking of soil, these plants prefer spe-cial mixes that suit their needs. African Violets and Gloxinias will do best in African Violet soil, which includes more moss than normal potting soil to hold moisture, and a little more sand to increase drainage. Bromeliads prefer — what else? — Bromeliad mixture. Because many varieties of this plant grow on trees rather than in soil, this potting mixture is very porous to help water drain away quickly. Both of these special potting mixtures are available prepackaged at nurseries or garden shops, or you can ask the staff to mix you up a batch.

### Taking the Plant Out

First, water the plant about an hour before you repot. This helps keep the soil together and lessens shock to the plant. Spread out

---

## THE PERILS OF CLAY

Unglazed terra cotta pots are very popular. They have a simple, traditional look, but can make watering tricky. The clay is porous and, although it allows good aeration of the soil, it allows water in the soil to evaporate, which means plants may not get the moisture they need. Because most flowering plants like moist conditions, you need to check the soil more frequently to make sure it hasn't dried out. Plan on watering more often. You can also put the plant in a pan of water for about fifteen minutes, or until the clay has darkened in color. Do this every couple of months to quench a clay-footed plant's thirst!

some newspaper; you're going to make a bit of a mess.

When you're ready to remove the plant from its pot, use a little tenderness. Don't just yank. Spread your fingers over the soil, cradling the plant. Tip the pot upside down and tap it on the edge of a counter. The plant should fall into your hand. Keep tapping and gently wiggling the plant until it is free.

### Putting the Plant In

Pour a shallow layer of soil into the new pot and stick the plant in. The base of the plant, the point at which it grows from the soil, should sit about an inch lower than the pot's rim. Adjust the soil level if necessary. Once the plant's at the right level, add soil evenly all around it. Get the soil into tight

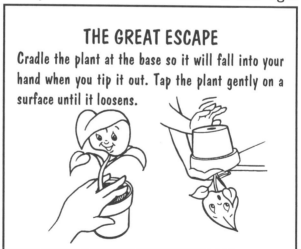

## THE GREAT ESCAPE

Cradle the plant at the base so it will fall into your hand when you tip it out. Tap the plant gently on a surface until it loosens.

spaces with a chopstick or screwdriver, avoiding any air pockets. Put a little fresh soil over the existing soil, but don't bury the plant's base. Press the plant firmly into the pot; but don't jam it in. If the soil's packed too tightly, water won't penetrate, and you'll have to pot it again. Give the plant a good drink of water, but don't fertilize for about a month to give the plant time to adjust to its new home.

# Propagating

### Oh, the Wonders of Nature

Propagating plants is a very cool thing. It's almost like cloning! You take a section of a mature plant and grow it into another plant. Since you can barely get many flowering houseplants to bloom a second time, it's not worth the effort to try propagating them. But you can propagate African Violets and Bromeliads. Here's how:

**Propagating African Violets.** There are two ways to create a new family of African Violets. The first method is by using leaf cuttings. Choose adolescent leaves; older and younger leaves won't have the energy or strength to survive breaking out on their own. Remove each leaf carefully, cutting the stalk at the base of the

plant. Trim the leaf stalk to about one and one-half inches.

Propagating from leaves can be tricky. Prepare several small pots with African Violet potting mixture; stick the leaf stalk in the soil at an angle, no deeper than one-half to three-quarters of an inch, just deep enough to stay in the soil. Keep the soil constantly moist. You may want to wrap the pot in a plastic bag or put a clear jar over the leaf to make a little greenhouse. This increases the humidity and keeps the newborn roots from drying out. After roots develop, tiny plantlets will appear at the base of the leaf. Cut away the parent leaf, leaving one plantlet in the pot, and plant the others in separate pots.

You can also root leaves in water. Fill a jar with lukewarm water (you've just cut the leaves away from Mother; no need to shock them with cold water) and cover the top with plastic wrap. Punch little holes in the plastic and stick the leaf stalks in the holes. This keeps them from falling into the water or out of the jar. The roots and small plantlets will form under water. Delicately separate plantlets from the mature leaf and put them in soil.

You can also propagate African Violets by dividing the plant's crown. Take a close look at the plant before removing it from its pot. If you only see one rosette of leaves coming up from the soil, it probably can't be divided. But if you see several distinct rosettes, you can separate these and plant them individually. Take the plant out of the pot and look at how the center of the plant is divided. You may need to carefully tease or rinse away some of the soil to see this. Gently tear apart the sections. Some may be connected by a thick umbilical cord root; cut this away with a sharp knife. Plant each of the sections and watch them grow!

**Propagating Bromeliads.** There's a poignancy to Bromeliads. They send out fascinating, colorful flowers and leaves — and die after the show is over. But they don't leave without a legacy. Bromeliads send up little offshoots, or "pups," from the soil. These are baby plants that can be separated and potted. Remove the mature plant from its pot and carefully separate the pups, cutting any umbilical cord root with a sharp knife. Plant the pups in Bromeliad potting mixture. Remember that Bromeliads are slow growers, and may take years to mature and bloom. If you don't have the patience, buy another mature plant.

### Child Rearing is a Long Process

Have patience when propagating plants. It can take anywhere from three to six weeks for a leaf cutting to develop roots, and then it will begin life as a growing plant. Baby plants also need a little while to adjust to the shock of separation and make the transition to being independent. Avoid feeding propagated plants for at least several months; you can overfertilize them and burn the young roots. Once the plant seems established and has been actively growing for at least several weeks, you can slowly build up to a regular feeding schedule over several months.

## Pests and Diseases

### Mayday! Mayday!

It's no fun to be under attack by a mess of angry hornets or a nasty stomach flu. Plants don't like bugs or diseases any more than we do. Houseplant pests and diseases usually aren't our fault, so there's no need to blame yourself. (Unlike when you try to knock a hornets' nest from under the eaves.) But just like when we're stung or sick, these situations require special care.

The Bloomin' Bunch is vulnerable to a few common pests and plant diseases. It's the price you pay for flowering beauty. Many of these plants are short-timers, so you won't have them around for too long. But it will only take a little while for a sick plant to infect other plants. Learn to recognize signs of pests and disease for these plants and check before you buy them. Here are some pests and diseases that can affect the Bloomin' Bunch.

### Aphids

These tiny bugs suck sap from stems and leaves of softer plants. Aphids can be green, black, brown, gray or light yellow. They multiply quickly and can be seen in masses on stems. Pick off by hand if a small infestation. Remove badly infected plant parts. Insecticides can also help.

### Fungus Gnats

Almost any plant can get gnats, sometimes called mushroom flies. These slow little bugs hover over the soil, but they aren't harmful. Systemic insecticide applied to the soil will control them.

### Scale

All plants are vulnerable to scale. When young, the brown or yellow insects move around the plant, but as they get older they develop a hard shell and cling like barnacles to leaves and branches. They suck sap and excrete a clear, sticky substance, a good sign they're around. Rub off with a swab dipped in rubbing alcohol, and remove badly infected parts. Insecticides also help.

### Leaf Miners

These are the tiny maggots of a small fly. They burrow between the surfaces of a leaf, sucking sap and creating patterns of irregular white lines on the leaf. These pests move fast and can quickly ruin a plant. Pick off damaged leaves, and treat plant with insecticide.

### Mealy Bugs

These white, quarter-inch bugs wrap themselves in a wool-like substance that repels water and contact insecticide. They suck sap and cause leaves to drop. Rub off with a swab dipped in rubbing alcohol, and remove badly infected parts. Systemic insect-icides can also help.

### Cyclamen Mites

These tiny bugs are so small you can't see them. Mites suck sap, causing leaves to curl and wrinkle and flowers to be distorted and fall early. You can use an insecticide to kill mites, but it's best to discard affected plants to avoid infecting other plants.

### Crown Rot

Soft and slimy spots on leaves caused by overwatering and low temperatures. The disease will eat leaves from the center outwards. An attack is usually fatal. Healthy leaves can be dusted with sulfur (available at nurseries) and propagated, but it's probably safer to discard the plant, buy another one, and watch the temperature and water.

### Gray Mold

A fungus caused by too much humidity creates a gray, fluffy mold on leaves and stems. Remove affected leaves, reduce humidity and avoid getting leaves wet.

### Powdery Mildew

Too much water or humidity, cool temperatures and poor air circulation can cause mildew, powdery white patches on leaves, stems and sometimes flowers. Affected leaves will twist up and fall off; in serious cases, all leaves will fall. Remove affected leaves and treat plant with fungicide.

Many pests can be destroyed by misting the plant with a solution of mild dish soap. Use about one-quarter to one-half teaspoon to one gallon of water. Cover the soil to protect it from soap, and rinse the plant well afterwards so the soap doesn't injure it. Do this once a week two or three times.

For plants that shouldn't get their leaves wet, use insecticides. Contact insecticides destroy pests and are sprayed onto the plants and bugs. Systemic insecticides work through the plant's sap and are applied to the soil or leaves. Insecticides are poisons; follow the label instructions carefully. If you're uncomfortable with insecticides, there aren't too many other options. It's better to start with a new plant than risk infecting all of your plants. Bring a sample of a sick plant to a nursery and ask the staff to determine the problem and recommend the best treatment.

> **plant fungicide:** this preparation fights fungal diseases such as mildew, and is sold at plant stores and nurseries.

# DECORATING WITH FLOWERING HOUSEPLANTS

### Just a Splash of Color

    With foliage houseplants, you decorate with the size and shape of the plant, the leaf texture and, for the most part, a lot of green. With flowering plants, your main decorating ingredient is color! No matter what style or hue your room is furnished in, a green plant will generally blend in comfortably. It won't be invisible, but it won't catch attention like the magenta blooms of an Indoor Azalea or a bright yellow pot of 'Mums. Flowering plants are like wearing an orange tie with a black tux — they get noticed. So how do you decorate with color as a focal point?

First, you may want to get something that complements the color and style of a particular room. If you've got a bright, sunny breakfast nook done up in warm yellow and red tones, a few Kalanchoes in vivid orange might perk up the family quicker than a double-shot of espresso. A quiet, formal sitting room decorated in grays and blues would be perfect for some traditional African Violets, or a few pots of white Chysanthemums. Those same 'Mums, only with maroon blossoms, might look great in a southwest-style room full of dark wood and earthy colors. Or maybe a Bromeliad with fiery pink bracts, to add the feeling of an Arizona sunset to your Ohio den.

### 'Tis the Season

You can also use flowering plants to decorate for the seasons. You can either complement them, or counter them. Try beating those cold wintertime blues with some sunny yellows — perhaps a couple of Kalanchoes to provide a spark, or maybe a bunch of 'Mums bright enough to recreate the sun right in your living room! Need to cool down that summer heat wave? Try a few African Violets in snowy shades of white and violet. If you want to complement the seasons, 'Mum blossoms in gold or rust will add a touch of

## A COOL PLACE FOR A NAP

NIGHT NIGHT!

Because many flowering plants like fairly cool temperatures at night, you may want to think about moving yours in the evening, especially if you do not set your thermostat at 55° when you go to bed. Check the evening temperature needs for your particular plant and see if there might be a spot that's cooler — maybe the basement or an enclosed porch. You don't have to get this involved, and even if you don't find the plant's ideal climate for an evening snooze, any decrease in temperature will help to prolong the life of the blossoms. So put out the cat, lock the door and set your blooming beauty in the pantry for the night.

autumn; white Azaleas will let you know spring is around the corner.

Don't think you have to limit yourself to one color of flower! A small grouping of pink and white Cyclamens, with their silvery green leaves, will look like a sweet cotton candy cloud atop a hill of Kentucky bluegrass. Three red Azaleas grouped around a white one will make their color seem ten times richer. The almost limitless hues of 'Mums can be used to create a patchwork quilt of color that perfectly suits your room or your mood.

### Don't Repot — Double Pot!

Most flowering plants are sold in plastic pots. They do the job; you don't have to change them. If a plant's only going to be around for a few weeks or months, there's certainly no sense in repotting it. But there are some things you can do to give short-time flowering plants a seat that's worthy of their noble beauty.

A simple white ceramic pot or pickle crock will elegantly highlight a plant's foliage and colorful blooms. A woven basket can provide a warm contrast for a showy plant, and can help it fit better in a more casual room. Some baskets are painted white, again to put the focus on the flowers. Be creative! Take that crystal bowl Aunt Ruth gave you for your wedding down from the attic and put a Rieger Begonia in it. Or get whimsical and have some fun. Grab that old milk pail out of the barn and put a white Azalea in it.

With all of these options, just stick the plant and its original pot in the new container. Keep an eye on closed containers to make sure drainage water isn't building up, and for porous containers like baskets, line them with aluminum foil to keep the water in its place.

Don't be shy about showing off the Bloomin' Bunch! If you've got company coming, set your Gloxinias in the center of the dining table. Put the African Violets on the white tablecloth with the cheeses and paté. Or stagger your Kalanchoes with tall candles to increase their fiery glow. Flowering plants are always dressed to impress, so make an impression!

## SOME INSPIRATION

- Group different colored 'Mums in front of the fireplace during the summer.
- Put a few Cyclamens in a large wicker basket on a counter.
- Line a narrow, white wall shelf with a collection of African Violets.
- Showcase a Bromeliad in a brushed metal bowl on a glass coffee table.
- Put Azaleas in an entryway to give visitors a bright welcome.
- Add a pot of color where it's least expected, like the bathroom counter.

## A Final Word

Decorating isn't rocket science or engineering; it's an art. A very personal one at that. There are no hard and fast rules. You know what you like. If a plant feels right, if the color makes you want to make a joyful noise, then it's the right plant for your home.

• • •

Flowering houseplants are nature's special treat. And even though some of them are short-lived, they don't need to be like that expensive box of chocolates that's always gone too soon. Just give them the right amount of water and light, and you can enjoy most flowering plants for weeks, if not months. With a precious few, the treat never ends.

For years, poems and sonnets and songs and paintings have been created to honor flowers. Have you ever looked at a flower closely, and felt that, even with all our technology, no manufactured item could possibly match its pure and simple beauty? If you have, then you understand the magic of flowers. If you haven't, do it soon. Then buy the plant and enjoy it every day in your own home. In fact, buy two. You deserve an extra treat.

# BIBLIOGRAPHY

Brookes, John. ed. *House Plants*. RD Home
Handbooks. Pleasantville, NY:
The Reader's Digest Association Inc.,
1990.

Graf, Alfred Byrd. *Exotica*. E. Rutherford,
NJ: Roehrs Co., Inc., 1973.

Handyman's Houseplants Tips Page. World
Wide Web, 1997.

Horticulture and Home Pest News. World
Wide Web. Ames, IA: Iowa State
University Extension, 1996.

"Plant Answers." *Aggie Horticulture*. World
Wide Web. College Station, TX: Texas
A&M University, 1997.

Seddon, George. *The Mitchell Beazley
Pocket Guide to Indoor Plants*. London,
England: Mitchell Beazley Publishers,
1979.

Taylor, Norman. *Taylor's Guide to
Houseplants*. Rev. ed. Boston, MA:
Houghton Mifflin Co., 1987.

*Time Life Houseplant Pavilion*. World Wide
Web. New York, NY: Time Life, Inc.,
1997.

# INDEX